Champions'Wisdom in 111 Sports Quotes for Young Boys

Champions' Wisdom in 111 Sports Quotes for Young Boys

Empowering Tomorrow's Heroes with Enduring Lessons from Sporting Legends

Aria Capri Publishing Group
Devon Abbruzzese & Mauricio Vasquez

Toronto, Canada

Authors:

Aria Capri Publishing Group
Devon Abbruzzese & Mauricio Vasquez

First Printing: November 2023

ISBN-978-1-990709-93-7

Who We Are at Aria Capri Publishing?

Hi there! We're Mauricio and Devon, the husband-and-wife team behind Aria Capri Publishing. Like any parents, we want the best for our family, and that's what we aim to give you through our books.

We both come from immigrant families, and we were brought up knowing how important it is to work hard, live well, and help others. These lessons from our own childhoods are what drive us to create books that can make a real difference in your family's life.

Our adventure in book-making started with the birth of our daughter, Aria Capri. She's the reason we jumped into this, and she's why we're so passionate about making sure our books have a positive impact. We even named our company after her!

If you're looking for books that are fun, educational, and good for your kids' growth, you've come to the right place. To check out our books, just scan this QR code.

Devon & Mauricio

Introduction

Hey there, young champion!

Embark on an exhilarating journey where words are as dynamic as a game-winning goal and as inspiring as a champion's endurance! This book isn't just a collection of quotes; it's a playbook of wisdom, guiding you to think bravely, dream boldly, and embrace the spirit of sportsmanship.

Why a book of sports quotes, you wonder? Picture this: having a special sports bag filled with advice from the greatest athletes and coaches ever. Whenever you need motivation, a boost of courage, or a spark of inspiration, just reach in and find the perfect words to fuel your passion.

These quotes are more than just words; they're like a high-five from your sports heroes, encouraging you to leap higher, run faster, and aim further. As you explore the thoughts of legends like Michael Jordan, or Serena Williams, it's as if they're right there with you, coaching and cheering you on.

But it's not just about their words—it's about what these words mean for you. That's why each quote in this book comes with a simple explanation to help you understand and apply it to your life. Whether it's about winning, losing, or playing with heart, these lessons are about lighting a fire in your mind, stirring your ambition, and making your day a bit more extraordinary.

Remember what Pele, the soccer legend, said? "Success is no accident. It is hard work, perseverance, learning, studying, sacrifice and most of all, love of what you are doing or learning to do."

We've gathered some of the most motivating and impactful quotes in sports, and now we're thrilled to share them with you.

So, are you ready to lace up your shoes and step into this arena of inspiration? Let's turn the page and kick off this adventure. Who knows? You might just be the next sports legend in the making!

Let's go, young champion!

Hey, Superstar Reader!

Picking up this book is like stepping into a legendary stadium filled with the secrets to success, teamwork, and maybe even a touch of sports magic. Here's why it's awesome:

Train Your Mind and Body: The inspiring quotes in this book are like coaching tips that can build strong muscles of knowledge and character in your mind.

Feel the Champion Spirit: These quotes are like teammates who get you. They can lift your spirits when you're down and help you understand the winning attitude.

Time-Out for Reflection: Reading a quote can be like a strategic time-out during a game—it helps you pause, reflect, and regain your focus.

Discover Your Inner Champion: It's like going on a scouting mission within yourself. You'll uncover new strengths and learn more about what makes you a great player and person.

Team Bonding: Sharing these quotes with your family is like a great team huddle. It strengthens your bond and gets everyone motivated.

Game-Changing Thoughts: Every quote is a chance to think like a coach, strategize like a player, and see the world from the perspective of sports legends.

Explore the World of Sports: These quotes are like a global sports tour, giving you insights into different games, and the power of sportsmanship.

Develop Winning Strategies: You'll learn how to tackle challenges, both on and off the field, and come up with smart plays to handle tough situations.

Dream Like a Champion: Let these words be the wind in your sails, driving your dreams to reach the heights of Olympic podiums.

For Every Young Athlete: Whether you're just getting into sports or you're a seasoned young athlete, there's wisdom here for everyone.

Parents, this book is a playbook for life, a catalyst for inspiring talks, and a support for your child's dreams and sportsmanship. It's perfect for every young athlete who loves to ask, "How can I get better?" and "What does it take to be a champion?"

So, are you ready to lace up your shoes, step onto the field, and discover some of the most motivating, powerful words ever spoken by sports heroes? Let's jump in!

Parents, We need your support!

Have you ever thought about the power of a simple act of kindness? One that doesn't cost anything and only takes a moment of your time?

Imagine this: Right now, there's a parent just like you looking for ways to inspire their child, to spark their imagination, and to guide them through life's ups and downs. They're searching for resources to help their child grow, dream, and become the best they can be. Your insights on this book could light the way for them.

Reviews are more than words; they are the shared experiences, the wisdom passed on, and the trust that binds us. If this collection of inspirational quotes has touched your family's life, would you consider leaving a review?

Your perspective could:
- Help another parent discover the perfect tool for bedtime stories that teach and comfort.
- Guide a family to resources that support their child's emotional and intellectual growth.
- Provide a spark of inspiration that might otherwise have been overlooked.
- Contribute to the positive development of a child in another household.

By sharing your thoughts, you're not just leaving a review; you're helping to weave a tapestry of community support. And if these quotes have resonated with you and your little ones, think about passing this book on. Introducing someone to a resource that could change a child's perspective is a gift that keeps on giving.

We're deeply grateful for your choice to bring our book into your home. Thank you for considering extending that warmth and support to others.

With heartfelt appreciation,

Devon & Mauricio

QUOTES

1. "You miss 100% of the shots you don't take." - Wayne Gretzky (Hockey)

   What it means: Even if you're nervous, give things a try! Whether it's talking to someone new or trying a tricky puzzle, you won't know what's possible unless you take that chance. It's all about being brave and giving it a go, no matter what.

2. "The mind is the limit. As long as the mind can envision the fact that you can do something, you can do it." - Arnold Schwarzenegger (Bodybuilding)

   What it means: Your brain is super powerful. If you can dream of doing something cool, like scoring a goal or acing a test, believe in it, and you can really make it happen. It's all about what you think you can do.

3. "Courage doesn't mean you don't get afraid. Courage means you don't let fear stop you." - Bethany Hamilton (Surfing)

   What it means: It's normal to feel scared, like when trying a new sport or speaking in front of class. Being brave means doing these things even when you're scared. Your courage is stronger than your fear!

4. "A champion is someone who gets up when he can't." - Jack Dempsey (Boxing)

   What it means: A real winner isn't just someone who never falls; it's someone who gets back up every time, even when it's really hard, like after losing a game or making a mistake.

5. "I am building a fire, and everyday I train, I add more fuel. At just the right moment, I light the match." - Mia Hamm (Soccer)

   What it means: Every day you practice or learn something new, you're getting ready for a big moment to show your skills. It's like getting ready to light a big, bright fire of success!

6. "Don't let what you can't do stop you from doing what you can do." - John Wooden (Basketball Coach)

   What it means: Focus on the things you're good at. Maybe there are things you find hard, but there are also things you're great at. Do those things and do them well!

7. "The only one who can tell you 'you can't win' is you and you don't have to listen." - Jessica Ennis-Hill (Track and Field)

   What it means: Sometimes, you might think you can't do something, like finish a big project or win a race. Remember, you don't have to listen to that doubt. Believe in yourself and give it your all!

8. "Never let your head hang down. Never give up and sit down and grieve. Find another way." - Satchel Paige (Baseball)

   What it means: If things don't go as planned, like if you lose a game or don't do well on a test, don't be too sad. Look for a new way to try or a different solution.

9. "Persistence can change failure into extraordinary achievement." - Matt Biondi (Swimming)

   What it means: Keep trying, even if you fail at first. Your continuous effort can turn a failure into something really amazing, like finally learning to swim or mastering a tricky game.

10. "Winning isn't everything, but wanting to win is." - Vince Lombardi (American Football Coach)

    What it means: It's important to want to win, like trying your best in a race or a test. That desire to succeed shows your determination and spirit.

11. "The highest compliment that you can pay me is to say that I work hard every day." - Wayne Gretzky (Ice Hockey)

    What it means: Being known for working hard, in school or sports, is a great thing. It means you're always giving your best effort!

12. "You can't put a limit on anything. The more you dream, the farther you get." - Michael Phelps (Swimming)

   What it means: Dream as big as you can! Whether you're thinking about swimming, running, or becoming a scientist, your dreams can take you far.

13. "I've failed over and over and over again in my life. And that is why I succeed." - Michael Jordan (Basketball)

   What it means: Making mistakes is okay. Every time you try and fail, you learn something new. That's how you get better and succeed!

14. "Age is no barrier. It's a limitation you put on your mind." - Jackie Joyner-Kersee (Track and Field)

   What it means: You're never too young to achieve big things. Don't let your age stop you from trying new sports or learning new skills.

15. "It's not the mountains ahead to climb that wear you out; it's the pebble in your shoe." - Muhammad Ali (Boxing)

   What it means: Sometimes, it's the small problems that make things difficult. Solving little challenges can make the big ones easier.

16. "To give any less than your best is to sacrifice the gift." - Steve Prefontaine (Distance Runner)

    What it means: Always do your best. You have amazing talents and abilities, so don't hold back – use them well!

17. "I hated every minute of training, but I said, 'Don't quit. Suffer now and live the rest of your life as a champion.'" - Muhammad Ali (Boxing)

    What it means: Training can be tough, but it's worth it. It prepares you to be a champion in sports, school, and life.

18. "The only way to prove that you're a good sport is to lose." - Ernie Banks (Baseball)

    What it means: It's important to be a good sport, even when you lose. It shows you can be happy for others and that you're brave.

19. "You have to believe in yourself when no one else does - that makes you a winner right there." - Venus Williams (Tennis)

    What it means: Believing in yourself is key. Even if others doubt you, your belief in yourself can make you a winner.

20. "It's not over till it's over." - Yogi Berra (Baseball)

What it means: Don't give up until the end, whether it's a game or a tough task. You never know what can happen!

21. "The harder the conflict, the more glorious the triumph." - Thomas Paine (Historical Figure, included for its athletic relevance)

What it means: When you work hard through tough times, like a difficult game or problem, winning or solving it feels amazing.

22. "Never say never because limits, like fears, are often just an illusion." - Michael Jordan (Basketball)

What it means: Don't limit yourself. Often, what you're afraid of doing isn't as impossible as you think.

23. "One man practicing sportsmanship is far better than 50 preaching it." - Knute Rockne (American Football Coach)

What it means: Being a good sport, like playing fair and being kind, is more important than just talking about it.

24. "The strength of the team is each individual member. The strength of each member is the team." - Phil Jackson (Basketball Coach)

What it means: You and your team make each other stronger. Whether in sports or group projects, everyone makes a difference.

25. "Set your goals high, and don't stop till you get there." - Bo Jackson (Baseball and American Football)

What it means: Aim for big dreams and keep going until you reach them. Whether it's a high score in a game or doing well in school, don't stop trying.

26. "When you've got something to prove, there's nothing greater than a challenge." - Terry Bradshaw (American Football

What it means: Challenges are your chance to show how great you can be. Take on tough tasks with confidence!

27. "A champion is afraid of losing. Everyone else is afraid of winning." - Billie Jean King (Tennis)

What it means: Being a champion means you worry more about not giving your best than about winning. Always aim to do your best.

28. "The more difficult the victory, the greater the happiness in winning." - Pelé (Soccer)

What it means: When you work super hard for something, like winning a soccer match or acing a test, it feels even more awesome when you succeed.

29. "It is not the size of a man but the size of his heart that matters." - Evander Holyfield (Boxing)

What it means: It's not about how big or strong you are. What really matters is how brave and kind you are inside.

30. "The only person who can stop you from reaching your goals is you." - Jackie Joyner-Kersee (Track and Field)

What it means: You can achieve big things! Believe in yourself and don't let your own doubts hold you back.

31. "You can't put a limit on anything. The more you dream, the farther you get." - Michael Phelps (Swimming)

What it means: Dream as big as you can! Whether it's swimming, studying, or space travel, your dreams can lead you to amazing places.

32. "It's not about perfect. It's about effort." - Jillian Michaels (Fitness Trainer)

What it means: Trying your best is what matters, not being perfect. Every effort you make is a step towards doing great things.

33. "Continuous effort - not strength or intelligence - is the key to unlocking our potential." - Winston Churchill (Statesman, included for athletic relevance)

What it means: Keep trying, even if it's hard. It's your effort and persistence that help you learn and grow.

34. "The only way to prove that you're a good sport is to lose." - Ernie Banks (Baseball)

What it means: Being a good sport, like cheering for others and playing fair, shows true character, especially when you don't win.

35. "Do you know what my favorite part of the game is? The opportunity to play." - Mike Singletary (American Football)

What it means: Enjoy playing and being part of a team. Winning is fun, but playing the game and doing your best is what's really important.

36. "Never let the fear of striking out keep you from playing the game." - Babe Ruth (Baseball)

What it means: Don't be scared to try. Whether it's baseball or answering a question in class, it's better to try and miss than never to try at all.

37. "Winners never quit, and quitters never win." - Vince Lombardi (American Football Coach)
What it means: Keep going and don't give up. Whether it's in sports, school, or a hobby, never quitting is what makes you a winner.

38. "Excellence is not a singular act but a habit. You are what you repeatedly do." - Shaquille O'Neal (Basketball)

What it means: Being excellent comes from doing your best all the time. Practice, study, and kindness should be your everyday habits.

39. "The only disability in life is a bad attitude." - Scott Hamilton (Figure Skating)

What it means: A positive attitude is super important. It's not what you can't do that matters, but what you do with a smile and determination.

40. "It's not whether you get knocked down; it's whether you get up." - Vince Lombardi (American Football Coach)

What it means: When you fall or fail, the important thing is to get back up and keep trying. That's how you learn and get better!

41. "The harder the conflict, the more glorious the triumph." - Thomas Paine (Historical Figure, included for athletic relevance)

What it means: Hard work and overcoming challenges make success even sweeter. When you work hard, winning feels great!

42. "The only limit to our realization of tomorrow is our doubts of today." - Franklin D. Roosevelt (Former U.S. President, included for athletic relevance)

What it means: Don't let your doubts stop you. Believe in yourself, and you can make your dreams for tomorrow come true.

43. "The only one who can tell you 'you can't win' is you and you don't have to listen." - Jessica Ennis-Hill (Track and Field)

What it means: Don't let self-doubt hold you back. Believe in yourself, and you can achieve things that others might think are impossible.

44. "It's a slow process, but quitting won't speed it up." - Unknown (Attributed to various sports personalities)

What it means: Learning and growing take time. Don't give up, because quitting won't help you reach your goals any faster.

45. "Don't put a limit on anything. The more you dream, the farther you get." - Michael Phelps (Swimming)
What it means: Dream big dreams and work hard to make them come true. There's no limit to what you can achieve with determination.

46. "When you've got something to prove, there's nothing greater than a challenge." - Terry Bradshaw (American Football)

What it means: Challenges are opportunities to show how strong and smart you are. Face them with courage and determination!

47. "One man practicing sportsmanship is far better than 50 preaching it." - Knute Rockne (American Football Coach)

What it means: Being a good sport is about what you do, not just what you say. Show kindness and fairness in your actions.

48. "Set your goals high, and don't stop till you get there." - Bo Jackson (Baseball and American Football)

What it means: Aim for big things and keep working towards them. Whether it's a sport, a school subject, or a hobby, don't stop until you reach your goal.

49. "Age is no barrier. It's a limitation you put on your mind." - Jackie Joyner-Kersee (Track and Field)

What it means: No matter how young you are, you can achieve amazing things. Don't let age stop you from trying new things and reaching for your dreams.

50. "It's not the mountain we conquer, but ourselves." - Sir Edmund Hillary (Mountaineer)

What it means: The biggest thing you can overcome is not a physical challenge, like climbing or running, but learning to believe in yourself and overcome your own doubts.

51. "I've failed over and over and over again in my life and that is why I succeed." - Michael Jordan (Basketball)

What it means: Every time you make a mistake or don't win, it helps you learn and get better. That's how you become successful!

52. "If you can believe it, the mind can achieve it." - Ronnie Lott (American Football)

What it means: If you think you can do something, like scoring a goal or solving a hard math problem, you're halfway there. Believing is powerful!

53. "Champions keep playing until they get it right." - Billie Jean King (Tennis)

What it means: Keep practicing and trying, whether it's in sports, a game, or learning a new skill. Champions don't give up!

54. "You have to expect things of yourself before you can do them." - Michael Jordan (Basketball)

What it means: First, think that you can do something amazing. This belief in yourself is the first step to making it happen.

55. "The difference between the impossible and the possible lies in a person's determination." - Tommy Lasorda (Baseball Coach)

What it means: With enough determination, you can do things that seem impossible, like winning a tough game or acing a difficult test.

56. "The road to Easy Street goes through the sewer." - John Madden (American Football Coach)

What it means: To achieve your goals, sometimes you have to go through tough times, like working hard on your studies or training in a sport.

57. "The only way to overcome is to hang in." - Dan O'Brien (Decathlete)

What it means: When things get tough, the best way to succeed is to keep trying and never give up.

58. "To uncover your true potential you must first find your own limits, and then you have to have the courage to blow past them." - Picabo Street (Alpine Ski Racer)

What it means: Find out what you're capable of, and then push yourself even further to do even better.

59. "One man can be a crucial ingredient on a team, but one man cannot make a team." - Kareem Abdul-Jabbar (Basketball)

What it means: Being part of a team means everyone is important. You can make a big difference, but you need your teammates too.

60. "It's not the will to win that matters—everyone has that. It's the will to prepare to win that matters." - Paul "Bear" Bryant (American Football Coach)

What it means: Wanting to win is good, but being ready to win is what really counts. Practice and prepare to do your best.

61. "Do not let what you cannot do interfere with what you can do." - John Wooden (Basketball Coach)

What it means: Focus on the things you're good at and keep improving them. Don't worry too much about what's hard for you.

62. "Perfection is not attainable, but if we chase perfection, we can catch excellence." - Vince Lombardi (American Football Coach)

What it means: You don't have to be perfect, but if you try your best, you can achieve amazing things.

63. "It's not whether you get knocked down; it's whether you get up." - Vince Lombardi (American Football Coach)

What it means: Getting back up after you fall or fail is what counts. It shows how strong and brave you are!

64. "The only person who can stop you from reaching your goals is you." - Jackie Joyner-Kersee (Track and Field)

What it means: Believe in yourself! You can achieve your dreams if you don't let your own doubts stop you.

65. "You can't control the wind, but you can adjust your sails." - Jimmy Dean (Country Singer and Businessman, quote included for its relevance in sports)

What it means: You can't change everything, like the weather or a test question, but you can change what you do, like how you prepare or play.

66. "It's not the will to win that matters, but the will to prepare to win that makes the difference." - Paul "Bear" Bryant (American Football Coach)

What it means: Wanting to win is great, but the effort you put into getting ready for it, like practicing and studying, is what really helps you succeed.

67. "The harder the battle, the sweeter the victory." - Les Brown (Motivational Speaker, included for its relevance in sports)

What it means: Tough challenges make success feel even more special. When you work hard, winning feels fantastic!

68. "Never let your head hang down. Never give up and sit down and grieve. Find another way." - Satchel Paige (Baseball)

What it means: If things don't go as planned, don't be too sad. Look for a new way to try or a different solution.

69. "Persistence can change failure into extraordinary achievement." - Matt Biondi (Swimming)

What it means: Keep trying, even if you don't succeed at first. Your continuous effort can turn a failure into something really amazing.

70. "The only way to prove that you're a good sport is to lose." - Ernie Banks (Baseball)

What it means: Being good at sports isn't just about winning. It's about how you act when you lose, showing kindness and being happy for others.

71. "You can't get much done in life if you only work on the days when you feel good." - Jerry West (Basketball)

What it means: To achieve great things, like finishing a big project or improving in a sport, you have to keep working even on days you don't feel like it.

72. "A trophy carries dust. Memories last forever." - Mary Lou Retton (Gymnastics)

What it means: Winning a prize is cool, but the fun and lessons you learn will stay with you much longer than any trophy.

73. "Obstacles don't have to stop you. If you run into a wall, don't turn around and give up." - Michael Jordan (Basketball)

What it means: When you face a challenge, like a hard homework problem or a tough game, find ways to overcome it instead of giving up.

74. "The most rewarding things you do in life are often the ones that look like they cannot be done." - Arnold Palmer (Golf)

What it means: The best achievements are the ones that seem too hard at first. When you succeed in these, it feels amazing!

75. "It is not the size of a man but the size of his heart that matters." - Evander Holyfield (Boxing)

What it means: Being brave and kind is more important than how big or strong you are. It's what's inside that counts.

76. "Success is where preparation and opportunity meet." - Bobby Unser (Auto Racing)

What it means: To be successful, like winning a race or doing well in a test, you need to be ready and grab the chance when it comes.

77. "Just keep going. Everybody gets better if they keep at it." - Ted Williams (Baseball)

What it means: Practice makes perfect. Keep trying, whether it's a sport, a hobby, or schoolwork, and you'll see improvement.

78. "I've learned that something constructive comes from every defeat." - Tom Landry (American Football Coach)

What it means: Every time you don't win, you learn something new. This helps you do better next time.

79. "To uncover your true potential you must first find your own limits, and then you have to have the courage to blow past them." - Picabo Street (Skiing)

What it means: Find out how good you can be at something, then push yourself even more to become even better.

80. "You miss 100% of the shots you don't take." - Wayne Gretzky (Ice Hockey)

What it means: You can't succeed if you don't try. Take a chance, like answering a question in class or trying a new sport.

81. "It's not whether you get knocked down; it's whether you get up." - Vince Lombardi (American Football Coach)

What it means: Falling or failing is part of learning. What matters is getting back up and trying again.

82. "The hardest part about being an athlete is going through times when you don't believe in yourself." - Brian Skrudland (Ice Hockey)

What it means: Sometimes, the toughest part is to keep believing in yourself, especially when things get hard. Always keep faith in your abilities.

83. "I learned that courage was not the absence of fear, but the triumph over it." - Nelson Mandela (Statesman, included for his athletic spirit)

What it means: Being brave doesn't mean you're never scared. It means you do things even when you are scared.

84. "You have to believe in yourself when no one else does - that makes you a winner right there." - Venus Williams (Tennis)

What it means: Believe in yourself, especially when others doubt you. Your belief is what makes you strong and a winner.

85. "A champion is someone who gets up, even when he can't." - Jack Dempsey (Boxing)

What it means: A true champion gets back up and keeps trying, no matter how tough it gets.

86. "The only limit to our realization of tomorrow is our doubts of today." - Franklin D. Roosevelt (Former U.S. President, included for his inspirational spirit)

What it means: Don't let today's doubts stop you. Believe in a brighter tomorrow and work hard to make it happen.

87. "The more difficult the victory, the greater the happiness in winning." - Pelé (Soccer)

What it means: When you work hard and overcome challenges, winning feels much more special. It's the hard work that makes success sweet.

88. "An athlete cannot run with money in his pockets. He must run with hope in his heart and dreams in his head." - Emil Zátopek (Long-Distance Runner)

What it means: It's not about having the fanciest equipment. It's your hopes and dreams that really help you run fast and achieve big things.

89. "Do not let what you cannot do interfere with what you can do." - John Wooden (Basketball Coach)

What it means: Don't worry about the things you find hard. Focus on what you're good at and keep getting better at it!

90. "Never let the fear of striking out keep you from playing the game." - Babe Ruth (Baseball)

What it means: Don't be afraid to try, even if you might fail. Whether it's playing a new sport or answering a question in class, the important thing is to participate.

91. "Hard days are the best because that's when champions are made." - Gabby Douglas (Gymnastics)

What it means: Tough days, like when training is hard or homework is challenging, are when you learn and grow the most. That's how you become great!

92. "You can't win unless you learn how to lose." - Kareem Abdul-Jabbar (Basketball)

What it means: Losing is part of learning to win. It teaches you to try harder and shows you how to improve.

93. "The only way to prove that you're a good sport is to lose." - Ernie Banks (Baseball)

What it means: When you don't win, being happy for the winner shows you're a good sport. It's about having fun and doing your best.

94. "It's not about the shoes, it's about what you do in them." - Michael Jordan (Basketball)

What it means: It's not about having the best gear. It's about how hard you try and what you can do with what you have.

95. "You have to believe in yourself when no one else does." - Serena Williams (Tennis)

What it means: Even if others doubt you, believing in yourself is what matters. Your belief can make you a champion.

96. "If you aren't going all the way, why go at all?" - Joe Namath (American Football)

What it means: If you're going to do something, like playing a sport or a school project, give it your all. Do your best!

97. "The more you dream, the more you achieve." - Michael Phelps (Swimming)

What it means: Big dreams can lead to big achievements. Dream about doing great things, and then work hard to make them happen.

98. "Do not let what you cannot do interfere with what you can do." - John Wooden (Basketball Coach)

What it means: Focus on the things you're good at, and keep improving them. Don't worry too much about what's difficult for you.

99. "It's not whether you get knocked down; it's whether you get up." - Vince Lombardi (American Football Coach)

What it means: Falling down or failing is okay. What's important is that you get back up and try again. That's how you learn and succeed!

100. "It's hard to beat a person who never gives up." - Babe Ruth (Baseball)

What it means: If you keep trying and never give up, like in a game or with a tough homework assignment, you can achieve amazing things.

101. "To give any less than your best is to sacrifice the gift." - Steve Prefontaine (Distance Runner)

What it means: Always do your best. You have special talents and skills, so use them fully and never hold back.

102. "A champion is someone who gets up when he can't." - Jack Dempsey (Boxing)

What it means: A true champion keeps going, even when things are really tough, like getting up after a fall or trying again after a mistake.

103. "Winning isn't everything, but wanting to win is." - Vince Lombardi (American Football Coach)

What it means: Wanting to win, like trying your best in a race or a test, is really important. It shows you're trying and you care.

104. "I've learned that something constructive comes from every defeat." - Tom Landry (American Football Coach)

What it means: Every time you don't win, you learn something that helps you do better next time. Every defeat teaches you something.

105. "The harder the battle, the sweeter the victory." - Les Brown (Motivational Speaker, included for its relevance in sports)

What it means: When you work really hard for something, like winning a sports match or finishing a big project, winning feels even more awesome.

106. "The only place success comes before work is in the dictionary." - Vidal Sassoon (Hairstylist, Entrepreneur, included for its relevance in sports)

What it means: To be successful, you have to work hard first. Success comes from effort and dedication, not luck.

107. "The difference between a successful person and others is not a lack of strength, not a lack of knowledge, but rather a lack in will." - Vince Lombardi (American Football Coach)

What it means: What makes you successful isn't just being strong or smart, it's having the will to keep trying and not give up.

108. "Only he who can see the invisible can do the impossible." - Frank L. Gaines (Motivational Speaker, included for its relevance in sports)

What it means: If you can imagine achieving something, you can make it happen. Believe in your dreams and work to make them real.

109. "It's not whether you get knocked down, it's whether you get up." - Vince Lombardi (American Football Coach)

What it means: It's normal to fail or fall sometimes. What's important is that you get back up and keep trying. That's how you improve and succeed!

110. "You have to train your mind as much as your body." - Venus Williams (Tennis)

What it means: Just like you practice sports, it's important to train your brain too. Think positively, study hard, and learn to face challenges. Your mind and body work together to help you do amazing things!

111. "It ain't about how hard you hit. It's about how hard you can get hit and keep moving forward." - Rocky Balboa (Fictional Character from "Rocky," Boxing)

What it means: Being strong isn't just about winning easily. It's about how you can face tough times, like a hard day or a big problem, and still keep going. Keep pushing forward, no matter what!

www.ingramcontent.com/pod-product-compliance
Lightning Source LLC
Chambersburg PA
CBHW011226120626
46545CB00010B/3169